100 facts
Birds

100 facts
Birds

Jinny Johnson

Consultant: Camilla de la Bedoyere

Miles
Kelly

First published in 2001 by Miles Kelly Publishing Ltd
Harding's Barn, Bardfield End Green, Thaxted, Essex, CM6 3PX

This updated edition published in 2014

6 8 10 9 7

Publishing Director Belinda Gallagher
Creative Director Jo Cowan
Editor Amy Johnson
Designers Rob Hale, Andrea Slane
Image Manager Liberty Newton
Production Manager Elizabeth Collins
Indexer Jane Parker
Reprographics Stephan Davis, Jennifer Cozens, Thom Allaway

ISBN 978-1-78209-585-9

Printed in China

British Library Cataloguing-in-Publication Data
A catalogue record for this book is available from the British Library

ACKNOWLEDGEMENTS
The publishers would like to thank the following sources for the use of their photographs:
Key: t = top, b = bottom, c = centre, l = left, r = right, m = main, bg = background
Cover (front) Dennis Stewart/National Geographic My Shot/National Geographic Society/Corbis,
(back, t) PhotonCatcher/Shutterstock, (bl) ariusz/iStock, (br) TMore Campbell/Shutterstock
Alamy 41(t) David Tipling **Corbis** 14–15(m) DLILLC; 14(b) Kevin Schafer; 36(t) John Carnemolla;
43(cr) Rick Price **Dreamstime** 11(t) Chmelars; 27(t) Thesmid; 37(b) Lukyslukys; 44(b) Steve Byland
FLPA 10(b) Kevin Elsby; 13(b) Roger Tidman; 16(b) David Hosking; 19(b) ImageBroker/Imagebroker;
30–31(m) Horst Jegen/Imagebroker; 32(b) ImageBroker/Imagebroker; 34(m) Jurgen & Christine Sohns;
35(t) Konrad Wothe/Minden Pictures; 39(b) Shem Compion; 43(t) Dieter Hopf/Imagebroker;
46–47(m) Terry Whittaker **Fotolia** 1 Stefan Andronache; 37(t, bg) pdtnc **iStock** 22–23(bg) ElsvanderGun
National Geographic Creative 17(cl) TIM LAMAN; 20(b) KLAUS NIGGE **NPL** 19(t) Mark Carwardine;
38(m) Rolf Nussbaumer; 45(cr) Andrew Walmsley **Shutterstock** 2–3 Captiva55; 5(tl, tc, tr) Eric Isselee,
(b) Rich Lindie; 6–7(m) Atul Sinai Borker; 8(t) Grant Glendinning, (l–r) Florian Andronache, Eduardo Rivero,
Eduardo Rivero, Clinton Moffat, (b, bg) nuttakit; 9(b) BMJ; 10(m) Sergei25, (b, bg) monbibi; 12(b) ktsdesign;
13(t) AndreAnita; 15(t) WayneDuguay; 16–17(t) Eric Isselee; 18–19 Alfredo Maiquez; 22(t) Gregg Williams,
(b) Arto Hakola, (tr, bl) Johan Swanepoel, (tl, br) monbibi; 23(cl) Johan Swanepoel, (b) monbibi;
25(t) tntphototravis, (b) Stu Porter, (bg) T.Allendorf; 26(m) Jerome Whittingham; 27(b) Kimberley McClard;
29(t) picturepartners, (b) IbajaUsap; 31(b) David Dohnal; 32(t) Gentoo Multimedia Limited; 33(t) Jan de Wild,
(b) Karel Gallas; 34(t, bg) monbibi; 35(bl) worldswildlifewonders, (br) worldswildlifewonders; 36–37
John Carnemolla; 37(panel, clockwise from tl) Anton_Ivanov, Eric Isselee, Jason Mintzer; 38(b) Richard Fitzer;
39(tl) zimmytws; 40 FloridaStock; 42–43 Rob McKay; 45(tl) fotofactory; 46(t) You Touch Pix of EuToch,
(t, b) monbibi; 47(t) monbibi **Superstock** 17(br) Biosphoto

All other photographs are from:
digitalSTOCK, digitalvision, John Foxx, PhotoAlto, PhotoDisc, PhotoEssentials, PhotoPro, Stockbyte

The publishers would like to thank Stuart Jackson-Carter for the artwork he contributed to this book.

All other artworks are from the Miles Kelly Artwork Bank

Every effort has been made to acknowledge the source and copyright holder of each picture.
Miles Kelly Publishing apologizes for any unintentional errors or omissions.

Made with paper from a sustainable forest

www.mileskelly.net
info@mileskelly.net

Contents

What are birds?

1 A bird has two legs, a pair of wings and a body that is covered with feathers. Birds are one of the types of animals we see most often in the wild. They live all over the world – everywhere from Antarctica to the hottest deserts. They range in size from the huge ostrich, which can be up to 2.75 metres tall, to the tiny bee hummingbird, which is scarcely bigger than a real bee.

▲ Baya weaver birds are found across South and Southeast Asia. As their name suggests, weaver birds build nests by weaving together strips of plant material and leaves.

The bird world

2 There are over 9000 different types, or species, of bird. These have been organized by scientists into 29 groups called orders, which contain many different species. The largest is the Passeriformes order.

▼ This chaffinch is in the Passeriformes order. More than half of all bird species belong to this order.

Wings

Crown

Bill, or beak

Throat

Passeriformes order: Includes robins, sparrows and wrens

Breast

Tail

Toes

Two legs

Common swift

Apodiformes order: Swifts and hummingbirds

Keel-billed toucan

Piciformes order: Toucans and woodpeckers

Blue-and-yellow macaw

Psitticiformes order: Parrots, cockatoos and lorikeets

Pied avocet

Charadiiformes order: Waders, gulls and auks

▲ The shape of a bird's beak can be used to decide which order a bird belongs to. These pictures show examples from the largest orders.

3 All birds have wings. These are the bird's front limbs. There are many different wing shapes. Birds that soar in the sky for hours, such as eagles, have long, broad wings. These help them use air currents. Small, fast-flying birds such as swifts have slim, pointed wings.

► Feathers have different shapes, sizes and textures, suited to the jobs they do.

Tail feather

Flight feather

Contour (body) feather

Down feather

4 Birds are the only creatures that have feathers. They are made of keratin – the same material as our hair and nails. Feathers keep a bird warm, and its wing and tail feathers help it to fly. Some birds have colourful feathers to help attract mates or blend in with their surroundings – camouflage.

5 All birds have a beak, or bill, for eating. The beak is made of bone and is covered with a hard material called horn. Birds have different kinds of beak for different types of food. Insect-eating birds tend to have thin, sharp beaks for picking up their tiny prey. The parrot's strong beak is ideal for cracking nuts. Hunting birds, such as goshawks, have powerful hooked beaks for tearing flesh.

6 Birds lay eggs. It would be impossible for birds to carry their developing young inside their bodies like mammals do – they would be too heavy to fly.

▼ The egg protects the growing chick and provides it with food. While the young develop, the parent birds, such as this common eider, keep the eggs safe and warm. This is called incubation.

Big and small

7 **The world's largest bird is the ostrich.** This long-legged bird stands up to 2.75 metres tall and weighs up to 115 kilograms – twice as much as an average adult human. Males are slightly larger than females. The ostrich lives mainly on the grasslands of Africa where it feeds on plant material such as leaves, flowers and seeds.

9 **The heaviest flying bird is the great bustard.** The male weighs about 12 kilograms, although the female is slightly smaller. The bustard is a strong flier, but spends much of its life on the ground.

▶ This male ostrich is looking after his chicks. Females are smaller than males and have brown feathers.

8 **The bee hummingbird is the world's smallest bird.** Its body, including its tail, is about 5 centimetres long and it weighs only 2 grams – about the same as a small spoonful of rice. It lives on Caribbean islands, particularly Cuba, and feeds on flower nectar like other hummingbirds.

10 **Wilson's storm petrel is the smallest seabird in the world.** Only 16–19 centimetres long, this petrel hops over the surface of the water snatching up tiny sea creatures to eat. It is very common over the Atlantic, Indian and Antarctic Oceans.

◀ A tiny bee hummingbird eats half its weight in food every day.

11 **The wandering albatross has the longest wings of any bird.** When outstretched, they can measure as much as 3.6 metres from tip to tip. The albatross spends most of its life in the air. It flies over the oceans, snatching fish and squid from the water's surface.

▲ The wandering albatross only comes to land at breeding time. It lays its eggs on islands in the South Pacific, South Atlantic and Indian Ocean.

12 **The largest bird of prey is the Andean condor.** A type of vulture, this bird measures about 110 centimetres in length and weighs up to 12 kilograms. It soars over the Andes Mountains of South America, hunting for food such as the remains of sheep, cows and llamas.

13 **One of the smallest birds of prey is the collared falconet.** This little bird, which lives in India and Southeast Asia, is only about 17 centimetres long. It hunts insects and other small birds.

► The collared falconet lives in forests. Its small size helps it to fly quickly between trees.

► Andean condors often perch in tall trees and on cliffs.

11

Fast movers

14 The fastest flying bird is the peregrine falcon. It hunts other birds in the air and makes spectacular high-speed dives to catch its prey. During a hunting dive, a peregrine may reach speeds of 200 kilometres an hour. In normal level flight, it flies at about 100 kilometres an hour. Peregrine falcons live almost everywhere in the world.

▶ When a peregrine falcon spots its prey, it enters into an incrediby fast, powerful dive, called a stoop.

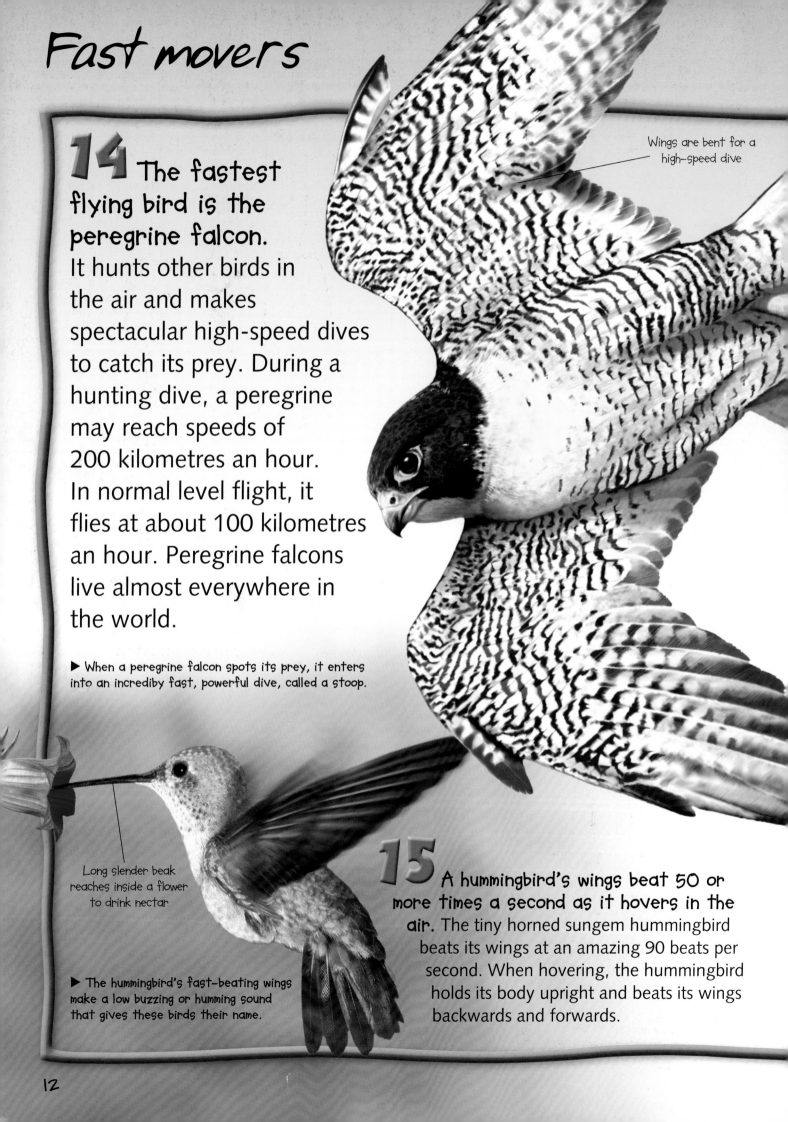

Wings are bent for a high-speed dive

Long slender beak reaches inside a flower to drink nectar

▶ The hummingbird's fast-beating wings make a low buzzing or humming sound that gives these birds their name.

15 A hummingbird's wings beat 50 or more times a second as it hovers in the air. The tiny horned sungem hummingbird beats its wings at an amazing 90 beats per second. When hovering, the hummingbird holds its body upright and beats its wings backwards and forwards.

16 Ducks and geese are also fast fliers. Many of them can fly at speeds of more than 65 kilometres an hour. The red-breasted merganser and the common eider duck can fly at up to 100 kilometres an hour.

Large, fan-shaped tail

▲ The male common eider has a distinctive patch of green feathers on the back of its neck.

17 The swift spends nearly all its life in the air and rarely comes to land. After leaving its nest, a young swift can fly up to 500,000 kilometres, and may not come to land again for two years. The common swift has been recorded flying at 112 kilometres an hour.

Swifts have long, slim wings that are perfect for their life in the air

▲ The swift can eat, drink, catch prey and mate on the wing.

18 The greater roadrunner is a fast mover on land. It runs at speeds of up to 27 kilometres an hour as it hunts for insects, lizards and birds' eggs to eat. It can fly but seems to prefer running or walking.

FEED THE BIRDS!

You will need:
225g of fat (suet, lard or dripping)
500g of seeds, nuts, biscuit crumbs, cake and other scraps   a piece of string

Ask an adult for help. Melt the fat, and mix it with the seeds and scraps. Pour it into an old yogurt pot and leave it to cool and harden. Remove the 'cake' and make a hole through it. Push the string through the hole and knot one end. Hang it from a tree, and watch as birds flock to eat it.

Superb swimmers

19 Penguins are the best swimmers and divers in the bird world. They live mostly in and around the Antarctic, at the very south of the world. They spend most of their lives in water, where they catch fish and tiny animals called krill to eat, but they do come to land to breed. Their wings act as strong flippers to push them through the water, and their tail and webbed feet help them to steer. Penguins sometimes get around on land by sliding over ice on their tummies!

▼ King penguins regularly dive to around 50 metres, but will sometimes go as deep as 300 metres, especially when food is scarce.

20 The gentoo penguin is one of the fastest swimming birds. It can swim at up to 36 kilometres an hour – faster than most people can run! Mostly, though, penguins probably swim at about 5 to 10 kilometres an hour.

▶ Gentoos race to shore then leap onto land using the surf to help them 'fly'.

21 The gannet makes an amazing dive from a height of 30 metres above the sea to catch fish. This seabird spots its prey as it soars above the ocean. Then with wings swept back and neck and beak held straight out in front, the gannet plunges like a dive-bomber. It enters the water, seizes its prey and surfaces a few seconds later.

▲ As a gannet plunges into water it must keep its eyes focused on its fast-moving prey.

QUIZ

1. Where do penguins breed – on land or in the water?
2. How fast can a gentoo penguin swim?
3. How deep do king penguins regularly dive?
4. From how high does a gannet dive?

Answers:
1. On land
2. Up to 36 kilometres an hour
3. Around 50 metres 4. 30 metres

Looking good

22 At the start of the breeding season male birds try to attract females. Some do this by showing off their feathers. Others perform special displays. The male peacock has a train of colourful feathers. When females come near, he spreads his tail, displaying the beautiful eye-like markings. He shakes the feathers to get the females' attention.

23 The male nightingale sings his tuneful song to attract females. Courtship is the main reason why birds sing, although some may sing at other times of year. A female nightingale chooses a male for his song rather than his looks.

▲ A male peacock displays his beautiful feathers. Females tend to choose males with the most attractive feathers and complicated patterns.

24 The male bowerbird attracts a mate by making a structure of twigs called a bower. He spends many hours making it attractive, by decorating it with berries, flowers and other objects. Females choose the males with the prettiest bowers. After mating, the female makes a nest for her eggs. The male's bower is no longer needed.

◀ The floor of this bird's bower is decorated with stones and plastic objects left behind by people.

26 The male roller performs a special display flight to impress his mate. Starting high in the air, he tumbles and rolls down to the ground while the female watches from a perch. Rollers are brightly coloured insect-eating birds.

I DON'T BELIEVE IT!
Water birds called great crested grebes perform a courtship dance together. During the dance they offer each other gifts – beakfuls of water weed!

27 Male cocks-of-the-rock dance to attract mates. Some of the most brightly coloured birds in the world, they gather in groups and leap up and down to show off their plumage to admiring females. They live in the South American rainforest.

▼ Male cocks-of-the-rock fight to win a female's attention.

◄ A dazzling display by the male will hopefully impress a female blue bird of paradise.

25 The blue bird of paradise hangs upside-down to show off his feathers. As he hangs, his tail feathers spread out and he swings backwards and forwards while making a special call to attract the attention of females. Most birds of paradise live in New Guinea. All the males have beautiful plumage, but females are much plainer.

28 **The barn owl is adapted for hunting at night.** Its large eyes are sensitive to dim light. Its ears can pinpoint the tiniest sound and help it to find prey. The fluffy edges of the owl's feathers soften the sound of wing beats so it can swoop silently.

▼ With its pale feathers, the barn owl is a ghostly night-time hunter.

The wings are held high as the bird reaches to grab its prey

29 **Some birds, such as the poorwill, hunt insects at night when there is less competition for prey.** The poorwill sleeps during the day and wakes up at dusk to start hunting. As it flies, it opens its beak very wide and snaps moths out of the air.

An owl's clawed feet are called talons

30 **Like bats, the oilbird of South America uses sounds to help it fly in darkness.** As it flies, it makes clicking noises that bounce off obstacles in the caves in which it lives, such as the cave walls, which help the bird find its way. At night, the oilbird leaves the caves to feed on the fruits of palm trees.

The tail is tipped forwards to slow the bird as it lands

▶ There are fewer than 200 kakapos alive in the world.

31 **The kakapo is the only parrot that is active at night.** During the day the kakapo sleeps in a burrow or under a rock, and at night it comes out to eat fruit, berries and leaves. It cannot fly, but it can climb up into trees using its beak and feet. The kakapo only lives on a few islands off the coast of New Zealand.

32 **Unlike most birds, the kiwi has a good sense of smell that helps it find food at night.** Using the nostrils at the tip of its long beak, the kiwi sniffs out worms and other creatures hiding in the soil. It plunges its beak into the ground to reach its prey.

QUIZ

1. What's special about the barn owl's feathers?
2. Can the kakapo fly?
3. Where are the kiwi's nostrils?

Answers:
1. They have fluffy edges 2. No 3. At the end of its beak

▶ The kiwi cannot fly. It is active at night, hunting for prey with its long, slender bill.

Home sweet home

33 Birds make nests in which to lay their eggs. The bald eagle makes one of the biggest nests of any bird. It is made mainly of sticks and is built in a tall tree or on rocks. It is used year after year. It can be as large as 2.5 metres across and 3.5 metres deep – big enough to fit several people!

▲ A male great hornbill brings food to his mate while she incubates the eggs.

34 The female hornbill lays her eggs in prison! After finding a big enough tree hole, the female seals herself inside. She blocks the entrance to the hole with mud, leaving only a small opening. The female looks after the eggs and the male brings food, passing it through the opening.

◄ Young bald eagles rely on their parents to feed them until they are several months old.

▼ A male weaver bird often builds his nest above water. He may build more than one nest, because he can have several mates.

② Then he makes a roof, and an entrance so he can get inside

③ When it's finished, the long entrance helps to provide a safe shelter for the eggs

① The male weaver bird twists strips of leaves around a branch or twig

35 The male weaver bird makes a nest from grass, stems and leaves. He knots and weaves the pieces together to make a long nest, which hangs from the branch of a tree. The nest makes a warm, cosy home for the eggs and young, and is also very hard for any predator to get into.

36 The malleefowl makes a temperature-controlled nest mound. It is made of plants covered with sand. As the plants rot, the inside of the mound gets warmer. The eggs are laid in the sides of the mound. The male keeps a check on the temperature with his beak. If the mound cools, he adds sand. If it gets too hot he makes some openings to let warmth out.

37 The cuckoo doesn't make a nest at all – she lays her eggs in the nests of other birds! She lays up to 12 eggs, all in different nests. The owner of the nest is called the host bird. The female cuckoo removes one of the host bird's eggs before laying one of her own, so the number in the nest remains the same.

38 The cave swiftlet makes a nest from its own saliva or spit. It uses the spit as glue to make a cup-shaped nest of feathers and grass.

21

Great travellers

39 The Canada goose spends summer in the Arctic and flies south in winter. This regular journey is called a migration. In summer, the Arctic blooms and there is food for the geese to eat while they rear their young. In autumn, when the weather turns colder, they migrate to warmer climates farther south. This means the bird gets warmer weather all year round.

Arctic

Southern North America

▶ Canada geese fly southwards before breeding.

▶ The Arctic tern travels farther than any other bird and sees more hours of daylight each year than any other creature.

Arctic

Antarctic

40 The Arctic tern makes one of the longest migrations of any bird. It breeds in the Arctic during the northern summer. Then, as winter approaches, the tern makes the long journey south to the Antarctic – a trip of some 15,000 kilometres – where it catches the southern summer. The tern gets the benefit of long daylight hours for feeding all year round.

▼ Some flocks of Canada geese make journeys of 1500 kilometres.

I DON'T BELIEVE IT!

Migrating birds can use landmarks, the position of the Sun when it sets and even the Earth's magnetic field to help them navigate.

Arctic tundra

Southern South America

▲ American golden plovers make some of the longest journeys of any animal.

41 Every autumn, the American golden plover flies up to 12,800 kilometres from North to South America. It breeds on the North American tundra where it feasts on the insects that fill the air during the brief Arctic summer. When summer is over the plover flies to the grasslands of southern South America for the winter. This means it has plentiful food supplies all year round.

Desert dwellers

42 The elf owl makes its nest in a hole in a desert cactus. This prickly, uncomfortable home helps to keep the owl's eggs safe from predators that do not want to struggle through the cactus' spines.

▶ The elf owl is one of the smallest owls in the world and is only about 14 centimetres long. It lives in desert areas in the southwest USA.

I DON'T BELIEVE IT!

The lammergeier vulture drops bones onto rocks to smash them. It then eats the soft marrow and even splinters of bone. Acids in the bird's stomach can digest the bone.

43 Desert birds may have to travel long distances to find water. This is not always possible for chicks. To solve this problem, the male sandgrouse has feathers on his tummy that act like sponges to hold water. He soaks his feathers, and then flies back to his young, which gulp down the water that he's brought.

◀ The sandgrouse lives throughout Asia, often in semi-desert areas.

44 Many desert birds have very light, sandy-brown feathers to blend with their surroundings. The cream-coloured courser lives in deserts in Africa and Asia. It searches for prey on the ground, as when it flies, the black-and-white pattern on the underside of its wings makes it easier for predators to spot.

◀ A cactus wren rarely needs to drink water. It can get most of what it needs from its food.

45 The lappet-faced vulture scavenges for its food. It glides over the deserts of Africa and the Middle East, searching for dead animals. The vulture attacks a carcass with its strong hooked bill. Its head and neck are bare so it does not have to clean its feathers after feeding from a messy carcass.

46 The cactus wren eats cactus fruits and berries. This little bird hops among the spines of cactus plants in search of juicy morsels. It also catches insects, small lizards and frogs. Cactus wrens live in the southwestern USA.

▼ The lappet-faced vulture is the largest vulture in Africa. It is strong enough to fight off other birds and even mammals such as jackals, and its large beak can rip through skin and muscle.

staying safe

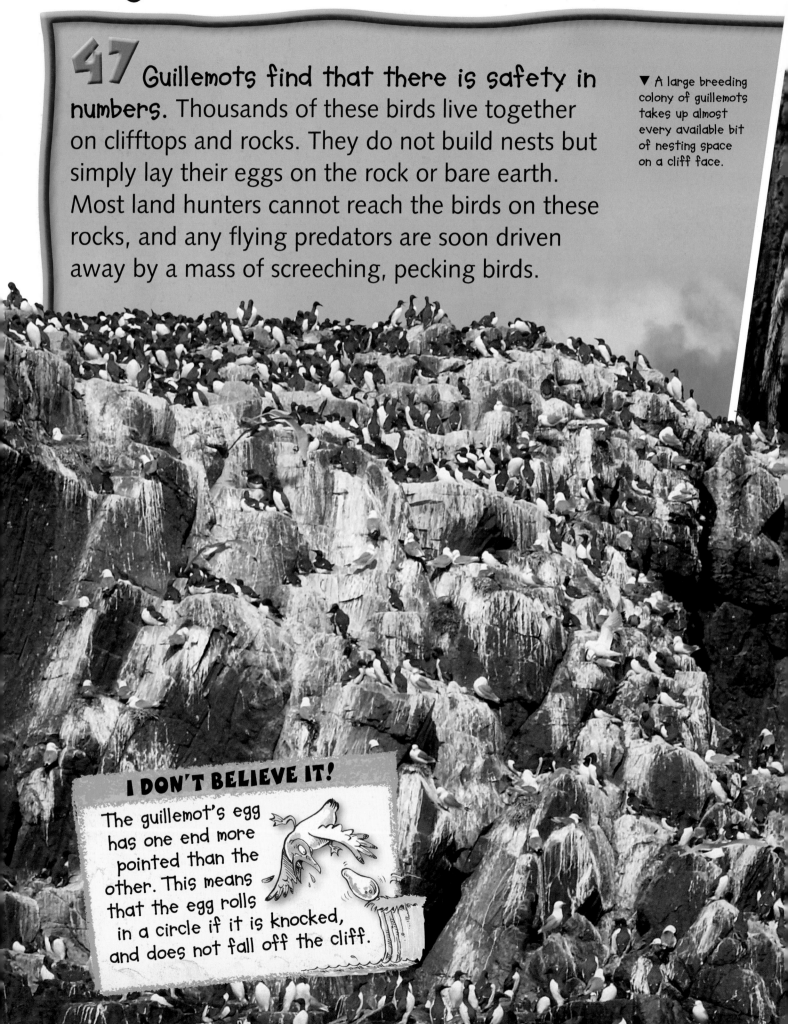

47 Guillemots find that there is safety in numbers. Thousands of these birds live together on clifftops and rocks. They do not build nests but simply lay their eggs on the rock or bare earth. Most land hunters cannot reach the birds on these rocks, and any flying predators are soon driven away by a mass of screeching, pecking birds.

▼ A large breeding colony of guillemots takes up almost every available bit of nesting space on a cliff face.

I DON'T BELIEVE IT!

The guillemot's egg has one end more pointed than the other. This means that the egg rolls in a circle if it is knocked, and does not fall off the cliff.

48 Birds have clever ways of hiding themselves from predators. The tawny frogmouth is an Australian bird that hunts at night. During the day, it rests in trees where its brownish, mottled feathers make it hard to see. If the bird senses danger it stretches itself, with its beak pointing upwards, so that it looks almost exactly like a broken branch or tree stump.

49 If a predator comes too close to her young, the female killdeer leads it away using a clever trick. She moves away from the nest, which is made on the ground, making sure the predator has noticed her. She then starts to drag one wing as though she is injured and is easy prey. When she has lead the predator far enough away, the killdeer suddenly flies away.

◄ Tawny frogmouths can blend in well, despite being large birds. They can grow to 50 centimetres long.

► A female killdeer imitates an injured wing to lead a predator away from her nest.

Amazing eggs

50 A bird's egg protects the developing chick inside. The yellow yolk in the egg provides the chick with food. Layers of egg white, called albumen, cushion the chick and keep it warm, and also supply it with food. The hard shell keeps everything safe. The shell is porous – it allows air in and out so that the chick can breathe. The parent birds incubate the egg in the nest.

51 The number of eggs laid in a clutch varies from one to more than 20. A clutch is the name for the number of eggs that a bird lays in one go. The number of clutches per year also changes from bird to bird. The grey partridge lays one of the biggest clutches, with an average of 15 to 19 eggs. The emperor penguin lays just one egg a year.

▼ The egg protects and nourishes the chick as it develops.

① The chick is beginning to form. It is nourished by the yolk.

Yolk sac contains food

② The chick's tiny wings and legs are beginning to grow.

Developing chick

Strong shell has pores (tiny holes) to allow air to pass through

③ Soon the chick's body will take up all the space inside the egg.

'Egg tooth'

④ The chick uses an 'egg tooth' to peck at the shell so it can hatch.

Egg white supplies proteins, water and vitamins

52 The ostrich egg is the biggest in the world. It weighs about 1.5 kilograms – an average hen's egg weighs only about 50 grams. The shell of the ostrich egg is very strong, measuring up to 2 millimetres thick. A female ostrich can lay up to 30 enormous eggs at a time. However, the ostrich egg is actually the smallest when compared to the size of the parent bird.

◄ An ostrich egg measures 16 centimetres in length.

53 The smallest egg in the world is laid by the bee hummingbird. The delicate egg is laid in a cup-shaped nest of cobwebs and plants. It weighs about 0.3 grams. The bird itself weighs only 2 grams.

ACTUAL SIZE

◄ The bee hummingbird egg is just 6 millimetres in length.

54 The kiwi lays an egg a quarter of her own size. The egg weighs 420 grams – the kiwi itself weighs only 1.7 kilograms. This is equivalent to a new human baby weighing 17.5 kilograms – most weigh about 3.5 kilograms.

55 The great spotted woodpecker incubates its egg for only ten days. This is one of the shortest incubation periods of any bird. The longest is of the wandering albatross, which incubates its eggs for up to 82 days.

QUIZ

1. Which part of the egg cushions the chick?

2. How many eggs a year does the emperor penguin lay?

3. How much does the bee hummingbird's egg weigh?

4. For how long does the wandering albatross incubate its eggs?

▶ A female great spotted woodpecker feeds a juicy caterpillar to her hungry chick. Once a chick has hatched it needs a lot of food.

Answers:
1. The egg white (albumen)
2. One 3. 0.3 grams
4. Up to 82 days

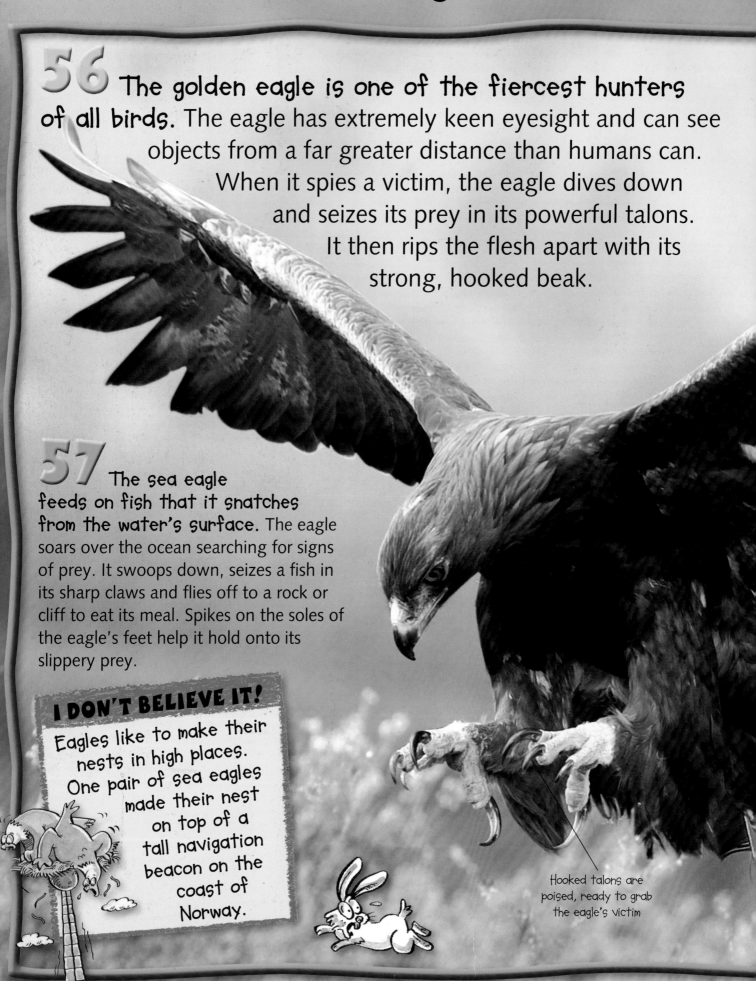

56 The golden eagle is one of the fiercest hunters of all birds. The eagle has extremely keen eyesight and can see objects from a far greater distance than humans can. When it spies a victim, the eagle dives down and seizes its prey in its powerful talons. It then rips the flesh apart with its strong, hooked beak.

57 The sea eagle feeds on fish that it snatches from the water's surface. The eagle soars over the ocean searching for signs of prey. It swoops down, seizes a fish in its sharp claws and flies off to a rock or cliff to eat its meal. Spikes on the soles of the eagle's feet help it hold onto its slippery prey.

I DON'T BELIEVE IT!

Eagles like to make their nests in high places. One pair of sea eagles made their nest on top of a tall navigation beacon on the coast of Norway.

Hooked talons are poised, ready to grab the eagle's victim

A single wing feather can be 35 to 50 centimetres long

◄ The golden eagle can soar for hours, searching for prey such as rabbits and other birds.

58 The raven is one of the biggest songbirds and a powerful hunter. It grows up to 63 centimetres long, has a strong beak and can run fast on the ground as well as fly. Rats and mice are its main prey, but it can even kill a creature as large as a rabbit. Ravens also scavenge, eating animals that are already dead or the kills of other hunters.

Tail feathers are unusually long – up to 35 centimetres

► Ravens look like crows, but their beaks are bigger and stronger.

Caring for the young

59 Emperor penguins have the worst breeding conditions of any bird. They lay eggs and rear their young on the Antarctic ice. The female penguin lays one egg at the start of the Antarctic winter. She returns to the sea, leaving her partner to incubate it on his feet. The egg is covered by a flap of the male's skin, which keeps it warm.

60 Hawks and falcons look after their young and bring them food for many weeks. Their chicks are born blind and helpless. They are totally dependent on their parents for food and protection until they grow large enough to hunt for themselves.

▶ When the chick hatches, the female penguin returns while the hungry male finds food. Emperor penguin chicks sit on their parents' feet to keep off the frozen ground.

▼ Peregrine falcon parents normally care for two to four chicks at a time.

61 Pigeons feed their young on 'pigeon milk'. This special liquid is made in the lining of part of the bird's throat, called the crop. The young birds are fed on this for the first few days of their lives and then start to eat seeds and other solid food.

62
Some birds, such as ducks and geese, are able to move around as soon as they hatch. Ducklings follow the first moving thing they see – usually their mother. This is called imprinting. It is a form of learning that can happen only in the first few hours of an animal's life. It ensures that the young birds stay close to their mother.

▼ These mallard chicks stand a greater chance of survival by staying close to their mother.

63
Young birds must learn their songs from adults. A young bird such as a chaffinch is born being able to make sounds. But, like a human baby learning to speak, it has to learn the chaffinch song by listening to its parents and practising.

64
Swans carry their young on their back as they swim. This allows the parent bird to move fast without having to wait for the young, called cygnets, to keep up. When the cygnets are riding on the parent bird's back they are safe from predators.

▼ A female mute swan and cygnets. Both parents take turns to care for the young.

Deep in the jungle

65 Birds of paradise are among the most colourful of all rainforest birds. The males have brilliant plumage and decorative feathers. There are about 42 different kinds and all live in the forests of New Guinea and northeast Australia. Fruit is their main source of food, but some feed on insects.

66 The scarlet macaw is one of the largest parrots in the world. It is an incredible 85 centimetres long, including its impressive tail, and lives in the South American rainforest. It moves in large flocks that screech as they fly from tree to tree, feeding on fruit and leaves.

◀ Parrots, such as the scarlet macaw, have hooked beaks that they use to crack nuts, open seeds and tear at fruit.

67 The junglefowl is the wild ancestor of the farmyard chicken. This colourful bird lives in the rainforests of Southeast Asia, where it feeds on seeds and insects.

▶ Hoatzins often live in small groups, and share the care of their chicks.

68 The hoatzin builds its nest overhanging water. If its chicks are in danger from predators they can escape by dropping into the water and swimming to safety. This strange bird with its ragged crest lives in the Amazon rainforest.

69 The Congo peafowl was only discovered in 1936. It lives in the dense rainforest of West Africa and is rarely seen. The male bird has beautiful glossy feathers of green, violet-blue and red, while the female is mostly brown and green.

▼ Harpy eagles perch on high branches to get a good view of the forest below.

70 The harpy eagle is the world's largest eagle. It is about 90 centimetres long and has huge feet and long, sharp claws. It feeds on rainforest animals such as monkeys and sloths.

◀ Quetzals can perch without moving a muscle, making themselves hard to spot in the rainforest.

71 The male resplendant quetzal has magnificent tail feathers, which are up to 90 centimetres long. This beautiful bird lives in the rainforests of Mexico and South America. It was worshipped as a sacred bird by the ancient Mayan and Aztec people.

Flightless birds

72 The fast-running emu is the largest bird native to Australia. Like the ostrich it cannot fly, but it can run at speeds of up to 50 kilometres an hour. Most flightless birds need speed to avoid being caught by predators. They have long legs, packed with muscles. Ostriches and emus can also deliver a mighty kick if they are scared.

▲ Emus can only run at top speed for a short time. They are hunted by wild dogs, eagles and crocodiles.

I DON'T BELIEVE IT!

One rhea egg is the equivalent in size to about 12 hen's eggs. It has long been a tasty feast for local people.

Very powerful upper leg muscles

Extra flexible ankles

▶ The ostrich is the world's fastest two-legged runner. It is specially adapted for speed, and can run at up to 70 kilometres an hour.

Penguins can waddle, run and jump, and are very strong swimmers

Kiwis rely on the cover of darkness, not speed, to stay safe

Roadrunners can reach speeds of 32 kilometres an hour, and they can also fly a little

▲ There are about 40 different types of flightless birds alive today, which have various ways of staying safe.

73 The speedy rhea lives on the grassy plains of South America. In the breeding season, males fight to gather a flock of females. Once he has his flock, the winning male digs a nest. Each of the females lays her eggs in this nest. The male incubates them, and looks after the chicks until they are about six months old.

▲ The rhea can sprint faster than a horse, reaching speeds of up to 50 kilometres an hour.

Long, strong legs

Bendy two-toed feet

74 Cassowaries are flightless birds that live in the rainforests of Australia and New Guinea. There are three species – all are large birds with long, strong legs and big, sharp-clawed feet. On the cassowary's head is a large horny crest, called a casque. Experts are not sure why cassowaries have casques, but they may be useful in making, and hearing, low booming calls that can be heard in the dense forest.

On the river

75 Kingfishers live close to rivers, where they hunt for fish. At breeding time, a pair of birds tunnels into the riverbank, using their strong beaks. They prepare a nesting chamber at the end of the long tunnel. Here the female can safely lay up to eight eggs. Both parents look after the eggs, and feed the chicks when they hatch.

► A kingfisher plunges into the water, grabbing a fish in its dagger-like beak.

▼ Ospreys are also known as 'fish hawks'. As they dive into the water, they keep the prey in their sights.

76 The osprey is a bird of prey that feeds mainly on fish. This bird is found almost all over the world near rivers and lakes. It watches for prey from the air then plunges into the water with its feet held out in front. Special spikes on the soles of its feet help it hold onto its slippery catch.

77 The pelican collects fish in the big pouch that hangs beneath its long beak. When the pelican pushes its beak into the water the pouch stretches and fills with water, scooping up fish. When the pelican lifts its head up, the water drains out of the pouch leaving the food behind.

▲ A pelican's massive pouch works like a fishing net to trap prey.

78 The jacana can walk on water! It has amazingly long toes that spread the bird's weight over a large area. This allows it to walk on floating lily pads as it hunts for food such as insects. Jacanas can also swim and dive. There are eight different types of jacana, also called lilytrotters.

79 The heron catches fish and other creatures such as insects and frogs. This long-legged bird stands on the shore or in shallow water and grabs its prey with a swift thrust of its sharp beak.

80 A small bird called the dipper is well-adapted to river life. It usually lives around fast-flowing streams and can swim and dive well. It can even walk along the bottom of a stream, snapping up prey such as insects and other small creatures. There are five different types of dipper and they live in North and South America, Asia and Europe.

▶ An African jacana feeds from water lettuce on the head of a hippopotamus.

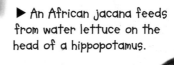

Finding food

81 The woodpecker uses its strong beak to bore into tree trunks and catch insects. The bird holds on to a tree trunk using its strong feet and sharp claws. Its stiff tail feathers also provide support. It hammers into the trunk, disturbing wood-boring insects that live beneath the bark. The woodpecker quickly snaps up the escaping insects.

◀ Woodpeckers also use their beaks to make nest holes in tree trunks, like this red-bellied woodpecker.

I DON'T BELIEVE IT!

The hummingbird has to eat lots of nectar to get enough energy to survive. If a human were to work as hard as a hummingbird, he or she would need to eat three times their weight in potatoes each day.

82
The antbird keeps watch over army ants as they march through the forest. The bird flies just ahead of the ants and perches on a low branch. It then pounces on the insects, spiders and other small creatures that try to escape from the column of ants. Some antbirds also eat the ants. Antbirds live in North and South America.

▲ Ocellated antbirds have a 'tooth' at the tip of the beak, for crushing insects.

83
The honeyguide bird uses the honey badger to help it get to its food. Found in parts of Africa and Asia, the honeyguide feeds on bee grubs and honey. It is not strong enough to break into bees' nests, so it leads the honey badger towards them. When the honey badger smashes into the nest, the honeyguide can also eat its fill.

84
The hummingbird feeds on flower nectar. Nectar is a sweet liquid made by flowers to attract pollinating insects. It is not always easy for birds to reach, but the hummingbird is able to hover in front of the flower while it sips the nectar using its long tongue.

▲ Colourful flowers and sweet perfumes attract nectar feeders, such as hummingbirds.

Winter birds

85 **The coldest places on Earth are the Arctic and the Antarctic.** The Arctic is at the most northern point of the Earth, and the Antarctic is at the far south. The snowy owl is one of the largest birds in the Arctic. Its white feathers help to camouflage it in the snow.

Dark bars on a female's feathers help her to hide when she is nesting among snowy rocks

86 **Penguins have a thick layer of fat just under their skin to help protect them from the cold.** Their feathers are waterproof and very tightly packed for warmth. Penguins live mainly in Antarctica, but some live in parts of South Africa, South America and Australia.

▶ Snowy owls ambush their prey, approaching with almost silent wing-beats.

87 **In winter, the ptarmigan has white feathers to help it hide from predators in the Arctic snow.** But in summer its white plumage would make it very easy to spot, so the ptarmigan moults and grows brown and grey feathers instead.

Winter plumage

Summer plumage

◀ Rock ptarmigans are stocky birds that feed on plants at ground level.

▲ Bewick swans care for their young throughout their first winter, and sometimes for a second winter too.

88 The Bewick swan lays its eggs and rears its young on the tundra of the Arctic. The female bird makes a nest on the ground and lays up to five eggs. Both parents care for the young. In autumn the family travels south to warmer lands.

89 Sheathbills are scavengers and will eat almost anything they can find. These large white birds live on islands close to the Antarctic. They do catch fish but they also search the beaches for any dead animals. They will also snatch weak or dying young from seals and penguins.

▼ A sheathbill tries to steal food from a gentoo penguin feeding its chick.

90 The snow bunting breeds on Arctic islands and farther north than any other bird. The female makes a nest of grasses, moss and lichens on the ground. She lays four to eight eggs and both parents help to care for the young.

Snowy owls have a wingspan of about 130 centimetres

Special beaks

91 The snail kite feeds primarily on water snails, and its curved beak is specially shaped for this diet. When the kite catches a snail, it holds it in one foot while standing on a branch or other perch. It strikes the snail's body with its sharp beak and shakes it from the shell.

▲ The snail kite is a type of hawk that lives in the southern USA, the Caribbean and South America. It is now very rare.

92 The lower half of the skimmer's beak is longer than the upper half. The skimmer flies just above the water with the lower part below the surface. When it comes across a fish, the skimmer snaps the upper part down to trap its prey.

93 The crossbill has a very unusual beak that crosses at the tip. This shape helps the bird to open up the scales of pine cones and remove the seeds that it feeds on.

◀ Male crossbills are red. Females are usually olive green or greenish-yellow, although both have dark brown wings and tail.

▶ There are sieve-like plates on the edges of a flamingo's beak. These plates help to trap the food that the bird eats.

94 The flamingo uses its beak to filter food from shallow water. It stands in the water with its head down and its beak beneath the surface. Water flows into the beak and is pushed out again by the flamingo's large tongue. Tiny animals and plants are trapped – and swallowed.

▼ This female wrybill can use her beak to reach young insects that lurk beneath pebbles.

95 The wrybill is the only bird with a beak that curves to the right. The wrybill is a type of plover that lives in New Zealand. It sweeps its beak over the ground in circles to pick up insects.

96 The toco toucan's beak is about 19 centimetres long. It helps the toucan to reach fruit and berries at the ends of branches. All toucans have large brightly coloured beaks. The different colours and patterns may help them attract mates.

▲ As well as a way of eating fruit, scientists think that a toucan's large beak may help it to lose heat when the bird is too hot.

Birds and people

97 People buying and selling wild birds has led to some species becoming very rare. Some pet birds, such as budgerigars, are bred in captivity but others, such as parrots, are illegally taken from the wild. The hyacinth macaw, which used to be common in South American jungles, is now rare due to people catching it to sell.

▶ There are fewer than 7000 hyacinth macaws left in the wild.

98 In some parts of the world, people still keep falcons for hunting. The birds are trained to kill animals and bring them back. When the birds are taken out, they wear special hoods to keep them calm. These are removed when the bird is released to chase its prey.

◀ Falconry – the practice of hunting with trained birds of prey – is one of the oldest sports in the world.

99 Many kinds of birds are reared for their eggs and meat. Chickens and their eggs are a major food source in many countries, and turkeys, ducks and geese are also eaten. Some wild birds, such as pheasants, are also used for food.

100 Starlings are common city birds. Huge flocks are often seen roosting on buildings. Starlings originally lived in Europe and Asia but were introduced to other countries. For example, in 1890, 60 starlings were released in New York City, followed by another 40 in 1891. Now starlings are among the most common birds in North America. The starling is very adaptable. It will eat a wide range of foods, and will nest almost anywhere.

▼ A huge flock of starlings such as this in Brighton, UK, makes a spectacular sight. One flock can number up to 100,000 birds.

I DON'T BELIEVE IT!

Urban-living crows drop walnuts amongst traffic. The cars break the shells as they move. The crows wait by crossings, and when the lights change to red, hop into the road to pick up the kernels!

Index

Page numbers in **bold** refer to main subject entries. Those in *italics* refer to illustrations.